Father Frans van der Lugt

Cultural, existential and psychological topics

Michel FRANCIS

Father Frans van der Lugt

Cultural, existential and psychological topics

Volume I

The artist **Fairouz TLAY** drew the portrait for this book.

Ms. Sheila Carroll corrected this text.

To those whom the thought of Father
Frans allowed a change towards a more
pleasant life.

ACKNOWLEDGEMENTS

I warmly thank the RCOAK Foundation and their management.

A BIOGRAPHY OF
FATHER FRANS

Frans van der Lugt was born in The Hague, the Netherlands, on April 10th, 1938.

He was the third of seven children, five boys and two girls. He was happy in the family circle where he received love and his faith.

At the age of eight or nine, he experienced for the first time in the church near his home the pure and unconditional love of God.

At the age of twelve he moved with his family from The Hague to Amsterdam, where the family settled down. As a young man he had a love affair with a young girl, which lasted for some time and brought him happiness. He felt, however, that a deeper desire was calling him to consecrate his heart, soul and mind to the love of God, to be a brother to all people. His vocation, so clear and precise, then took shape.

The two young people went through a long process of preparation for the break-up. Father Frans recounts this difficult moment:

«The morning I entered the novitiate, we had a drink in one of the most romantic places in

Amsterdam and we parted with a frank handshake». (Paul BEGUEYB S.J, Frans van der Lugt S.J, Bridge Builder and Martyr in Syria, Valkhof Pers, 2015, p. 19-20)

Frans also recounts a beautiful memory when he announced to his parents his decision to enter the Jesuits:

«It was February 2nd, 1959, the day before my father and mother were to celebrate their 25th wedding anniversary. That evening I happened to be in the living room, alone with my parents: "Dad and Mom, as an anniversary present, I want to give you etc." I shared my vocation with them. At first there was silence. Then I looked at my mother: a silent heart-to-heart meeting, of mother and son. Her eyes glowed, the deepest wish of her heart shone through in her gaze. Her gaze was transparent as glass, I looked at her heart as a believing mother who had prayed hard for one of her sons to become a priest. My father was standing next to her, as he always is: the man who has totally dedicated himself to his family and lived for them, deeply believing, fatherly, warm, calm. It was he who broke the silence and took a few steps towards me to congratulate me: "It is the most beautiful gift" It was one of those unforgettable moments. My parents suddenly became transparent to me. I understood even better their marital love and the place that children had in it». (Paul BEGUEYB S.J, Frans van der Lugt s.j, Bridge builder and martyr in

Syria, Valkhof Pers, 2015, p. 20-21).

In 1959, at the age of 21, he entered the Jesuit novitiate in Grave in the Netherlands.

Between 1961 and 1964, he studied philosophy in Nijmegen in the Netherlands. His dissertation is entitled: "Guilt among young people".

Between 1964 and 1966, he studied Arabic at the Notre Dame de Délivrance Institute in Bikfaya, Lebanon.

In 1966, he began his work in Homs, Syria, at the Collège Saint Jean de Damascène, teaching French, arithmetic, religion and also working as a supervisor at the high school.

Between 1968 and 1972, he studied theology in Lyon-Fourvière, France and also obtained a degree in psychology at the University of Lyon. He then continued his studies in psychology at the State University of Lyon.

In 1971, he was ordained a priest at the church of Saint Luke in Amsterdam.

In 1972, he returned to Homs for research and fieldwork for his thesis.

From 1973 to 1974, he continued writing his thesis at the Residence of Saint Ignatius in Beirut, Lebanon.

In 1974, he left for his third year in Belgium.

In 1975, he returned to Lyon to complete his

thesis.

In 1976, he obtained his doctorate in psychology. The subject of his thesis was: "The image of the married priest and the celibate priest in the Lebanese-Syrian Maronite community".

Between 1976 and 1978, he was in Aleppo, Syria where he worked with the Christian Youth movement.

In 1978 he returned to the Netherlands for training in psychotherapy and psychoanalytic studies and obtained a diploma in psychoanalysis.

In 1979 he left Holland to go to Belgium, where he was trained in Zen and Yoga.

Between 1980 and 1987 he was again in Homs, Syria. There he began to give spiritual retreats and to go on hikes.

During the period 1987-1993, he was appointed superior of the Jesuits in Damascus. He began to give conferences every Saturday for CLC (The Christian Life Community) groups. Once a week, he presented a cultural program on Buddhist meditation and Yoga at the Tishreen swimming pool.

During this period, he wrote three books: "Love, Who are you?", "From failure to success", "Listening and love".

In 1991, he started to prepare the Al-Ard project.

In 1993, the Al Ard project was born. Al-Ard is located near the city of Homs (Al-Qusayr road), where there is a house for disabled people, a ceramics factory, a guest house, a house of prayer called "The House of Peace", a cellar and an agricultural center. Father Frans founded this project with the support of Mr. Abdel Masih Atia.

In 1995, he was appointed superior of the Jesuits in Homs.

In 2014, on April 7th, he was assassinated in Homs, Syria.

Main activities

Father Frans van der Lugt gave lectures for years in several cities in Syria. He organized and guided spiritual retreats and trained people in Zen and Yoga. He accompanied several CLC groups.

He organized Al-Massir (The Hike) to discover nature and Syria as well as to participate in an experience of meeting and living together with others who are different because of their religion, their country, their skin color, etc. The walk has been recognized by the Syrian Sports Federation as a sports activity.

PREFACE
BY FATHER JAN BRONSVELD S.J

For those who knew Frans van der Lugt, it goes without saying that it is worthwhile to make him better known. I personally knew Frans mainly as a companion in the Society of Jesus, the Jesuits, and especially in Lyon where we were both students of theology and Frans also of psychology. We lived in a small community of about five Jesuits, depending on the year. It was an intense and fraternal community life. We cooked together, played sports, and one person's friends were another's friends.

Like myself, Frans was one of the 35 Dutch Jesuits who, during a period from 1958 to 1968, were destined to work in one of the countries of the Jesuit Province of the Near East, which in our time meant Lebanon, Syria or Egypt. Most of us went with the intention of spending our whole life in these countries. Thus Frans spent his entire active Jesuit life in Syria since 1964 and, apart from a few years of study in France and Holland, until his death in 2014.

I knew Frans as a very rich person, active, open, optimistic, able to lead people, free from the rules that society or the Church sometimes imposed.

Much has been written about Frans, especially in the period after his death. And although he himself was not really a writer, there are still three books written by him and published in Arabic. These three books show that what interested him most of all was man and his relationships with others. The titles of these books speak for themselves: "Love, Who Are You?", "Listening and Love", and "From Failure to Success". But, in fact, in order to transmit what made him live, it was above all through life and through the spoken word that he did it.

Through the accompaniment of people, the spiritual retreats he led, the walks he organized which were "itinerant" retreats and the conferences he gave wherever he went, in Homs, Damascus, Aleppo or elsewhere in Syria, Frans played an important role in the lives of many people.

Since he is no longer physically with us, it is good to have some traces of all this. The present volume, which is intended to be the first book of a series, finds its sources in Frans' lectures, which are obviously nourished by his studies of philosophy, theology, psychology and by his spiritual and social life. It is Frans who speaks through the pen of the author of this book who has translated his words into English and passed them on.

I retain two characteristic points of Frans which are found at the beginning and at the end of this book. First, his answer to the question in the first chapter: Why do I like to live? Frans loved life and he says why. I like to live because I have discovered the beauty of life, the beauty of nature, but above all the beauty of people.

Then what he says in the last chapter about inner peace. He asks two questions: do we live in the past, do we live in the future or do we live in the present with its negative and positive sides? Can we find inner peace in the present? For him, it is a question of accepting ourselves with all our history and of freeing ourselves from all forms of slavery, from all that prevents us from living. This liberation is difficult. Some people want to achieve it alone by isolating themselves in silence and listening to themselves. But to live in silence and listen to oneself, one needs a framework, a silent environment that helps. The group is important or a friend with whom one can remain in silence. But in the end, inner peace is a gift, a gift from God, from God who is present in everyone.

These different elements can be found in Frans. While being very active, he had his moments of silence, alone or with others. His life shows us his faith, shows us that the spirit of God was present in him and that it is present in others and ultimately in everything.

This is what inner peace is all about: discovering that God is in everything.

Jan Bronsveld s.j

(Shubra, Cairo, November 5, 2021)

INTRODUCTION

Father Frans van der Lugt, cultural, existential and psychological topics, is the title of a series of volumes. In the first volume, we aim to highlight an important aspect of Frans' personality: the lecturer. This aspect appears through the numerous conferences that Father Frans gave during several years in several cities of Syria for young people and adults. These lectures, on the whole, aim at drawing man's attention to himself in order to better discover what is repressed in him and to know better his personality.

Father Frans' personality is characterized by a certain number of traits that allowed him to carry out his analysis:

- Western culture and Eastern culture: both cultures gave Father Frans the ability to find the right balance. For example, between individual and collective life, Father Frans tried to value the positive traits in each society, to make thoughts and reflections evolve in order to find the right place and to have a dynamic movement between what is lived and what is possible to live.

- A deep knowledge of the reality in the East: this knowledge has been accumulated over the years, real relationships and contacts with people of all communities and beliefs have been established.

- Creative listening: it gave Father Frans the opportunity to get to the heart of the issues, to analyze them with clarity and precision.

- Fr. Frans' solidarity with the people: he participated in their joys and sorrows with unconditional love. He also tried to find ways for people to cope with their difficulties.

- His mastery of the Arabic language and his facility in using many puns: they allowed him to clarify what he wanted to say and expose.

- His methodology in the analysis and his humor in the expression: they made his words enter the heart of the people.

In this first volume, we have chosen six themes, which are:

"Why I like to live? And why I do not like to live?"

"The difficulty of dialogue with oneself and with the other"

"From the mask to the truth"

"Freud and the interpretation of dreams"

"How do you live with fear and anxiety?"

"How do you find the inner peace?"

This work required modifying the Arabic

language, from dialect to a literary language while keeping the spirit of the text before translating it.

I. WHY DO I LIKE TO LIVE? WHY DO I NOT LIKE TO LIVE?

I like to live if I have discovered the beauty and the meaning of life.

I like to live if I see something beautiful in the present that takes me out of the past and into the future.

I like to live if I have a beautiful goal in my life and I want to achieve it with faith, patience and joy.

I like to live if I have discovered that I have value, that I am loved and loving.

I like to live if I have discovered in my life that there are people who love me, so I can be productive, creative and loving. So for me to love living, I have to discover the beauty of life.

After the last hike, someone who was with us said to me, "I took some beautiful pictures during the hike, do you want me to show them to you?"

I said, "Sure".

He showed me some very nice pictures. Indeed, this person has discovered the beauty of life in many simple areas. In the first picture, you can see a mountain here and a rock there. We see the mountain of Al-Aqraa and you can also see a small bird on a rock. He told me that he spent many hours to take this picture of the bird on the rock. Whoever looks at this picture sees, as I did, that this bird, alive, gives meaning and beauty to all of the nature around it, as if this bird on this rock is the master of the universe.

He showed me another picture. He explained to me that there was a rock here and a tree was growing next to it, then the tree broke, so a branch of the tree leaned over the rock as if it was embracing it. If a person contemplates this picture, the person, of course, contemplating the beauty of nature and see it, when looking at the branch embracing the rock as if it were a marriage between the branch and the rock

Anyone who contemplates such a photo could say that in our life there are difficulties, but we live in the hope of meeting a branch that embraces us and makes us feel that we are not all alone, it offers us the warmth of the embrace. This photographer saw the beauty and symbolism of this scene, but the majority of those walking saw nothing. Perhaps they were not free to see the beauty, but why? Is it because of fatigue and the desire to finish this hike, or is it because a love relationship was occupying their thoughts and was not allowing them to see this beauty?

I can say that the photographer gives his photograph and nature a moral and aesthetic value, as if he made the creation speak in the language of the Creator. Like the painter who paints the face of an old man; we can say that this face is a dead face, but the talent of the painter is to bring out from these almost dead wrinkles, a light from within that gives life to death.

If we also look at the Mystics, they have discovered the inner beauty of life and not the outer beauty. They stayed for many years in contemplation and silence until they discovered the divine dimension in the universe. This absolute and divine dimension illuminates all that is relative. Whoever discovers this light can see this light in everything, because from this light the creation came, this light is in the depth of the creation and not on the surface. Whoever enters the depth can discover this light.

It is not necessary that the person is a photographer or an artist or a mystic to discover and express the beauty of life. I believe that every person who frees his heart from his worries, and takes some time to look at nature, life, others and listen to the language of life could discover beauty and love life.

We do not always meet the artist or the mystic or the person who has discovered something beautiful in life. Usually, if we want to listen to people, they say that life is tasteless, that it is empty. It is a state of sadness. There are medicines in pharmacies against sadness to treat modern man in the East and in the West. Whoever sells medicines makes a lot of money but these medicines do not help to make dreams or films. There is sadness and despair in this age. There are also people who want to commit suicide, they told me, "Father, we are thinking of committing suicide after having suffered a severe shock in this life. But, if you want, we might not make this decision to commit suicide, so that God will not be displeased with us and will receive us after our death."

Whoever hears the words of these people, can classify them into five or more groups: people of routine, fanatics, consumers, victims of the cruelty of life and victims of psychological problems.

1. People of routine

A group of people says: In life, everything is routine, so nothing has color or taste. So the question arises: What is routine?

In Homs and outside Homs, sometimes in the night we take medicine to fall asleep. In the morning we say we have a headache and after breakfast we take medicine, then we go to work; then lunch and nap. After the nap we work or study again or go to the university and come home. Then we go out for a while and at ten o'clock in the evening we go home. We stay up or watch TV or a movie. Finally, we sleep.

So, what's new in this program of my life? Nothing! No creativity! When I live this program; my life is programmed from the beginning to the end, I cannot get out of this reality and hold my head high. I cannot say that I exist. I live like a sheep, but I am a creative person. I enjoy this life, but without the traditional, routine habits that frame it and lead to boredom, emptiness, repetition and sadness.

We address the older generation by saying: "Why do the kids not step out of these traditional, social, and religious customs to imagine new ways of doing things? You can live the way you want to live, do children have to be like sheep?".

The older ones answer: "If you want the truth, we do not have the strength or the enthusiasm to encourage our children to live their own lives."

You know that the disease of this age is the loss of strength and enthusiasm, all energies are wasted by routine. If I have some energy and I want to get out of this pagan vicious circle, I have to be inventive, there has to be an adventure, there has to be an initiative, but we are not used to doing that

To live a beautiful experience, I have to know myself and live a personal life with conviction. What should I do in my situation where I am more of a sheep than a human being?

If you ask me, I say: "You have to rebel a little, only a little. We have to know why we want to live".

Assuming that we have begun to live a personal life, our enthusiasm immediately wanes; fire does nothing by itself without wood. So we go back to our basics, to our habits as before, safe and sound.

If you start living differently, society will say: "Are you becoming different from others? ".

Jealousy starts here, it appears before the difference. If I were different from others in society, I would appear to them as having a skill that they lack. Because of jealousy, society pulls the person who wants to be different towards itself. The others force the person who wants to change to come back to be like the others. If he or she refuses, they judge, mock and ridicule him or her.

In irony, there is a sense of lack in the face of an abundance of difference, and the person desiring change feels a kind of isolation in the face of irony, because the person cannot tolerate being in a relationship with only a small group in society, a group that does not want to have a personal and creative experience. The man who wants to change and break the chains of society's captivity cannot bear to lose the good relationship with people and to think that society will reject his children as the society rejects himself. Finally, he submits again to the routine life, because this life is less hard than the creative life.

We see in the routine life the absence of a temporal, dynamic movement that gives meaning to life, to the past, the present and the future. Through the past, we come to the present and open ourselves to the future. We move into the future through the abandonment of the past. The problem is that there is only the past, the meager past, while the present is locked in the past and it is without a future.

When the past ties up the present without the possibility of opening it to the future, there is no meaning. And when the past captures the present and seizes it within itself, in this situation the present cannot be a future of the future and likewise the present cannot receive the past.

The person who is in this category of routine people, forces the present to remain within the past without giving it the possibility to be born and receive the light of the future.

2. The fanatics

They are those who live by the same principle: the past; the past kills the dynamics of life.

Who is the fanatic?

The fanatic has neither discovered the meaning nor the depth of life, he has not discovered the absolute in the dynamics of life.

The fanatic feels, unconsciously, that life has no essence and he addresses himself saying: I am in the abyss of death, but I do not wish to live in this abyss, I wish to fill it. What should I do because I have no real absolute and no real spirit?

I make a false absolute out of an event that covers the lack of a true absolute. I look for what is relative so that it becomes for me an absolute stronger than this fear of death. That is, I protect myself in a false absolutism against the danger of death. I then need ideas, specific religious practices, money or a position.

The fanatic, when he clings to an idea, clings violently for fear of losing it, because this idea has become for him the Absolute, the most important one, and it is difficult for him to lose it. That is why the attachment becomes violent, because if he loses this idea, he goes into the abyss of death.

It is dangerous to try to eliminate from this person his fanatical ideas because if he loses them, he loses his reason. Faced with this, he attacks and defends as much as he can and he also wants to get rid of the person who does not believe in his false absolutism. Let us take as an example what happened with Herod. He is fanatical about his function as king, because without this function he feels dead. He is very afraid of losing his position and if someone wants it, he loses his mind and becomes ready to kill that person instead of dying himself. The death of the other is permitted, but the idea of his own death is inadmissible to him

The fanatic does not like to live because he has not discovered an abundance of life so that he can love it. The fanatic does not like to die because he is afraid of death and he does not like to discover death in his life.

3. Consumers

They are those who live in the present without past and without future, in what sense?

They say that the past is gone and that a new event has come from the outside and eliminated everything from our past and therefore there is a present without a past. Where is the future? The future is ambiguous, so if we consider that the present is empty of the past and that the future is suspended in the air, then the past is empty and the present is also empty; so there is no value for the past and there is no possibility for the future.

If in the present time I have a little money, only a little, what can I do?

I will try to grasp directly what pleases me and therefore I want to consume this life, I have parties, trips, and go to restaurants, all in order to enjoy a direct relationship with the world. It is possible that the poor cannot live this consumption as much as the rich. Is the purpose of consumption to obtain the beauty of life? What is the meaning of life?

They tell you, "We do not have all the knowledge and the real knowledge is that the world is empty, without taste. What do you want us to do? Either we dive into the void and fall into death, boredom or repetition, or we cover or fill that void. What is better filling the void or living in it?"

It is possible to fill the void with religious matters, spiritual ritual, or fellowship, depending on the intelligence of the person. You go to these things not because of an inner force, but because of a desire to fill an inner void. You fill the void with religious matters and I with worldly matters. This method could work for a day, two days, a week, and then we come back and feel the emptiness again.

I can travel to France to fill this emptiness, then come back; after a week I feel like traveling again. Or without going far, here there are restaurants with delicious food, we eat greedily for a week and that allows us to abstain from eating for another week, then start eating again. So it is a consumer relationship that spoils what I get and does not offer me life. Food goes into the stomach and then comes out in a permanent consuming relationship. In the consumerist relationship, everything passes and nothing remains inside the heart.

In a consumerist relationship, I not only feel

that life is tasteless, but I feel that I am alone and my heart is empty, so I become sad. When I expect a lot from a person and what I do is consume him sexually and emotionally, then the person has not entered my heart; I have used him to satisfy my pleasure and need. Therefore, the result of the consumer system is a terrible isolation. What should we do? Hold gatherings?

In gatherings, I do not get anything essential. I can look at a person, the person look at me or admire my beauty and thus make me feel my value. The person could feel comfortable whenever there are many people around, it is an external relaxation, in which there is a demand for attention from the people around, because when I am alone with myself, I do not feel valued. Here, therefore, there is a problem in the group life: the fear that people do not visit me. If I do not visit people, they will not visit me, in this solitude I feel isolated and insignificant. All this, so that I am not rejected by others and do not live in isolation. How does the consumer system appear here?

The consumer does not distance himself from life to discover the beauty that is in it, he wants to consume life quickly, as he consumes goods for his needs, he does not listen to life and rather puts his hand on it to seize it and fill his void.

We can take physical beauty as an example. The body is beautiful in my opinion. Do I exploit it? Do I consume it? Or do I look at it and discover its beauty and its language? When my situation is consumerist, I want the other person's body to enjoy and it becomes a tool of pleasure to satisfy my sexual needs. I do not see the name of the one who has this body, I see it as a kind of food or a commodity. In consumerism, we ignore the body of the other, we deprive it of language and words, because it has become a tool of pleasure, and which cannot say anything. This is what pornographic films show. The fact of not communicating with the body, by words, creates a void, because there is no distance between us and it to listen to it. There is no distance for us to look at its beauty. These films are readily available, within our reach and we can watch them on television or satellite, on the computer, on the internet. In other words, if we want the body as a relationship of pleasure, we can find our demand in the consumable relationship with my body and the body of the other or with other bodies..

The question here is: why is there a strong sexual need that seeks to silence what is beautiful in the world and make the other feel like a meal?

The sexual need is not only a need for sex, it is much broader than immediate pleasure. Why is there a strong need?

I remember a poor person telling me, "I have a strong sexual need!".

In order to understand the reason, it is

necessary to understand the psychological background of sexual needs by listening to dreams.

I then asked him, "What do you dream?"

He replied, "I do not have dreams about sex, but I think about it a lot."

As if in the unconscious, there was a parameter more important than the sex, which makes the sex strong in the conscious

So I said to him, "What do you dream about?"

He said, "I dream that I am Napoleon and an important person like a head of state" In consciousness he feels a lack, a weakness and great powerlessness, and compensates for it in dreams where he sees himself as important.

If we want to understand the sexual drive here, we say that this man likes to have sex not only for the sake of sex, but it is possible that he feels that he has someone who cares about him. He is not impotent, but he feels insignificant and may look to sex for tenderness and the opportunity to find in a woman a sympathetic mother for him, for his lack, for his impotence and poverty. These reasons can lead to a strong sexual need.

The real need is not sex but the person, that is to say, the sex life becomes more and more necessary because we feel more and more that we are powerless, afraid of death and isolated. Isolation can make us want more movies to cope with it, but the result is that I feel more isolated and there is no relationship that controls the desire for consumption; the result, then, is depression and sadness. In order to eliminate these things, we proceed in the same way, so we do not solve the problem because it is much deeper than the superficial sexual need. We can say the same thing about the phenomenon of consumerism in this age, in the West and in the East, man feels a great emptiness and life has become an emptiness that has to be filled. We have not discovered life as an abundance, but we see it as empty. The question is: is there more sexual strength through greater consumption, is there more emptiness and a feeling of more helplessness and isolation? And did the people before us have the same feelings?

The people who were before us did not feel sex, the emptiness in the same way as we do, because they did not undergo major changes, they had a specific religious and social structure and habits. The past, the present and the future walked together in a coordinated way and there was nothing that entered the present to eliminate the past, there was no discontinuity with the past, but a kind of continuity and peace of mind.

Today, an external element violently enters the present, eliminates the past, and the impulse to project itself towards the future fades away. In Europe, today, it is the same thing. When we listen to the European youth, they say: "That globalization and technology are all there is to life. What do we want from the past? Why do we care about old concepts, about psychoanalysis and Freud? Religion, ethics, psychology and Greek or Latin culture, that is from the past. "

Nowadays, the mentality is like that. We discover that there is a discontinuity with the past and that there is no clear projection towards the future. The future will come without moral or psychological distinctions, is it good or not? And, the past, where is it?

Our past, in the East, is magnificent, there are very rich Arab customs, music, poetry, human values in relationships, values in the family unit, etc.! But today's children do not live much from the past, they live from external intrusive elements, which violently penetrate the present and make our past disappear immediately. For this reason, we feel that the past escapes us little by little and we are no longer aware of our future. As a result, we live in a more difficult situation.

What is the situation of parents who raise their children and who are not the product of the past and who have come from an external world and live according to the external concepts that enter the present?

It is possible that no era has experienced this rupture in a violent way, because there was no globalization. Globalization as a means is a good thing, but not when it becomes a false absolute that only tries to fill the void. The means becomes the absolute in the absence of the true in life, and globalization becomes a dangerous idolatry for man. The problem of emptiness exists in the East and in Europe and each society seeks to fill the emptiness in a way that seems appropriate to it.

I am able to fill the void of the present with the past and to fill the void of the present directly with consumption. We realize that people live a contradiction: on the one hand they do not like to live because they have not discovered an abundance in their life and the deep, absolute meaning. On the other hand, they do not like to die. The final death is the easiest because the person is put in the coffin and it is over. There are coffin sellers, like in front of the church in Umm Al-Zinnar, they wait for someone to die to sell a coffin. It is not a problem that the coffin sellers, priests and bishops earn some money from our death! But the problem is that the family becomes poorer. The subject here touches half the problem, the real problem is not death at the end of life, but death now at the height of life.

Failure and illness make me experience my limits and I also realize that there is an end to my life. So the question is: What do I have to do to pass from death to life, do I have an absolute that helps me to accept the moments of death in my life, or have I discovered nothing in my life stronger than death?

Here, death frightens me, not death at the end of my life because I will not feel anything after my death, but death in life, when I do not have a shore, towards which I go, to bypass my death. Death, therefore, haunts me and it is in front of me, in front of this reality, in front of the awful death I am terrified and I run away either in fanaticism, or in routine, or in consumption.

4. People who are victims of a cruel life

There are so many people who are victims of a cruel and vile life, what do they say?

They say that they have a small house, they do not have much money and they can't take the children out on the street because they do not know what will happen there. As a result, this family stays in the small apartment, on the fourth or fifth floor, with four, five or six children. These children can also be angry, annoying and difficult. The parents live in tension. How is it possible to live in this apartment? It is hell! The situation is very difficult and the most difficult thing is the lack of money; they wait for the end of the month and when they receive their money, they pay back their debts. There is   constant pressure in this life.

I admire these people and their patience, they endure the problems day after day. When you visit them and you hear the screaming, the problems, the dismay of the parents and you ask them about their situation, they say, "Everything is fine!"

If you tell these people, "Life is good, it has meaning, you should have fun and enjoy it," they will be angry at this language because it is far from their reality and does not fit in with their concerns.

When I tell them: "If man does not express what he lives and does not empty his heart, how can he contemplate the beauty of life and be happy?"

They answer: "We have the difficulty of bearing the problems of this life and you want us to contemplate the beauty of life. Those who go to meditate are people who seek to enjoy themselves, to see and contemplate themselves, not to meditate on the meaning of life. We want men supporting life and responsible, not children, not a meditation. "

What can we do to improve their situation so that they can have some free time?

I admire them for their patience, because they endure all this terrible suffering. They are much better than us. I hope their situation will improve without giving them any advice.

5. Victims of psychological problems

Victims of psychological problems are such a large group. In this category, people who suffered in their childhood and who cannot be freed from this pain because of its intensity are trapped in it.

This past blocks the present in the routine. Pain does not allow people who live in the present to open up to the future because they cannot accept the pain of the past.

I also admire the people who have endured these sufferings and have not committed suicide.

A few examples of this category, they are too numerous if we want to list them all.

The first example: The story of a young girl

This girl lives in a family, it consists of eleven girls and one boy. The boy, in this position becomes the absolute, a false absolute, he becomes everything and the girls have to put up with him.

If a girl dares and says that she works hard while he does nothing and sits like a prince on his throne, then the spoiled boy gets angry and throws his sister on the bed and wants to smother her. But the other girls take the boy away from their sister, then they tell the father that his son tried to strangle his daughter. The father says, "It's not a problem. We have many daughters. If one dies or lives, it's all the same."

When the girl hears this, she realizes that her existence has no meaning and that death is better.

She speaks up again, saying, "I went through this pain when I was fourteen years old, during my adolescence; if I do not express what I went through and share it with someone else to help me get out of this knot, then I will stay in it and my existence will remain meaningless."

So how can we ask this young girl to love the beauty of life and the meaning of life, when her existence, as a person, has no meaning or flavor?

The second example: childhood sexual abuse

Child sexual abuse leaves many problems, people try to hide this, but we need to talk in case of sexual abuse, because this abuse does a lot of harm to both the girl and the boy and because of this abuse, they lose trust in themselves and others, they grow up and live their lives in distrust. When I do not trust people and I do not trust life, it is impossible to find meaning in life.

The third example: failure in studies

Many young people, when they do not succeed in their studies, hear: "They do not understand anything and they aren't doing well at school".It leads to the following question: How do we want this person to have confidence in their life and discover its beauty if they themselves have not discovered it? We have to be careful when we address remarks to a child, because he does not distance himself from what is addressed to him in terms of judgments and images, he believes that he is as he has been described.

After exposing these five categories, we may enter into sadness, if we are not already there, or we enter into even greater sadness. We do everything we can to escape this harsh reality in various ways of anesthesia.

Life is beautiful when I discover the meaning of its beauty and my own value, when I know how to deal with the forms of death that exist at the heart of my life, because life and death are linked to each other. If I am afraid of death, I cannot love life. And the fundamental question is: What should I do with the death that exists in my life?

II. THE DIFFICUTY OF DIALOGUE WITH ONESELF AND WITH THE OTHER

We will first discuss the meaning of the word dialogue, and then we will deal with the difficulties of dialogue with the other, between the fiancée and the fiancé and between the wife and the husband.

1. The meaning of the personal way

We are born without having a personal word, "logos", we are born with a cry, which is not a person's own word. When the child begins to speak, he does not yet have a word "logos", because he does not express himself and his personal word is not yet formed. His words are a reflection of the words of his family and his surroundings. His own world has not yet given him the possibility of expressing himself in a speech. Since the child is not present through his words, we can say that he is like a mute. Whoever does not express himself by his own words remains mute. The one who talks is also mute, because he does not speak about himself.

After childhood, we grow little by little and so does our "self". Each child that is born has his own individuality as does the fetus. Each fetus has a dream that differs from the dream of another fetus, it is an unconscious dream. Consequently, each fetus is born with an individuality, but it is an unconscious individuality. This individuality does not become a word yet because it is until now in the unconscious.

When I begin to feel my feelings that could be unconscious, there is the possibility of their becoming a word, so all that is special in us enters in our "logos". Our human vocation is to incarnate by words all that is in us. All that is in us and that does not become a word does not give the possibility of a relationship with the other, because the relationship is generally built by words. Each time man grows in his humanity, the "logos", the personal word, develops more and more.

If I desire dialogue, I also desire a second "logos", a second word, that presupposes another person who has reached a maturity in his or her speech that allows for the construction of a dialogue. It is also difficult to find another person who expresses himself in a personal way, because in society we do everything to prevent the person from becoming "logos".

A person may not have dared to speak up and share their experience because people would laugh at them or not understand them. Thus, the person may not want to become a "logos", a word and therefore remains an image that conforms to what others expect and are satisfied with, because they are similar to them. However, if I want to be as others want me to be, I do not exist. When I am afraid to be a personal word, it is difficult to have a dialogue. The "dia" is the dynamic movement between two or more people, it is very important and it is positive, because it is the field of love between two people. The person who feels that he is a word is able to speak about himself and to ask for the listening of the other "logos". Above all, he must listen to his own words.

To listen, there must be a desire to receive the word of the other with attentive, loving ears and to take the right distance so that there is room for mutual movement, this field of "dia". The "dia" is a space between two "logos", between listening and speaking. When I listen to the word, the word becomes listening. The mutual movement allows the relationship to grow and reach its fullness.

In order to dialogue with the other, one needs a word that finds another word and one needs a positive field. This also applies to interreligious dialogue. When there is a field the "dia" of each religion remains peacefully in its particularity, in its own words, without fear, and feels that the difference with the other is an element that promotes peace.

In the course of our lives we experience the same thing, we all seek a relationship, but we realize that the relationship is very difficult.

2. The relationship in the engagement

Is there a personal word "logos" in the engagement?

Before the engagement, the person has not learned to be a word in which he expresses himself. The young woman was raised to speak a lot, saying, "I have many peculiarities, but I dare not confide them because the other is not worthy and I am shy. I am afraid that my words will be exploited and I am afraid of showing that I am weak when I express my feelings. For these reasons, I refrain from saying what I desire."

If her situation presents itself in this way during the engagement, that she cannot have a personal word, "logos", then the engagement for her becomes a mask, an image behind which the young woman hides.

As for the young man, he arrives at the engagement and sees himself as a person with reason and who knows how to think well. I do not know if the man thinks better than the woman, but the problem is that he comes to the engagement considering himself to be reasonable, without feelings or tenderness, because society shows the image of the man devoid of feelings, for this reason he represses his feelings and shows his masculinity. The young man does not express himself with his own words, but with the image that the society has of the man.

Therefore, in this engagement, we notice that there is no field to exchange a personal word between the woman and the man and that there is no listening; what is there? There are two images, an image of the fiancé and an image of the fiancée.

1.1 The image of the fiancé

It is the image of a visitor who visits his fiancée, if he does not do so, he suffers reproaches, because he must visit his fiancée every day. Moreover, he must be elegant, not wear sports clothes and he must pamper the bride-to-be. He must also be generous; if he is stingy, the family will not want him. When the groom invites the bride-to-be to a restaurant and spends a large amount of money, it is good, spending a small amount is not desirable.

If the fiancé has gone to America, he should call his fiancée at least four times a day. If he calls only once a week, there is criticism. The fiancé has every right to save money for the marriage instead of spending it on phone calls to show that he is generous!

He should not be economical with his words, when he visits his fiancée, he should tell jokes, that us how he should be.

1.2 The image of the bride-to-be

The bride-to-be is the one who waits, she waits

every day for the groom-to-be. She must be a virgin, otherwise the fiancé will leave her immediately. She must appear to the fiancé as spoiled and give him the opportunity to pamper her and she must be a little shy. In general, the bride-to-be is not shy, on the contrary, it is the groom-to-be who is shy. Overall, the fiancée tries to show that she is shy otherwise if her image shows that she is strong, he will leave her.

These are two typical engagement images among others. These two images do not express a personal word "logos" and there is no positive field "dia" between the two fiancés, because each is masked and there is no positive relationship when there are masks. Moreover, there is no possibility of meeting or development of the personality because of the presence of the mask and, finally, there is no development in the relationship with the other.

The question arises: is there an exchange of words and listening in the engagement?

The engaged couple sit together within a specific framework and it is not desirable that they both remain alone for a long time for fear of a few too many kisses. If the fiancé breaks off the engagement, the fiancée will be criticized by her family and by society. In an engagement, there is intense control, touching hands is sometimes a problem, always for fear that the engagement will be broken. For this reason, there is no exchange of personal words between the engaged couples because they sit together for a short time and must be chaperoned almost all the time. In this situation, each of them has to present only a beautiful image for the other to see, so the "dia" field between them does not exist.

We say to the engaged couple: "It is good to get to know each other and to know one another's history as well as their psychological, social and spiritual dimensions. It is necessary to know each other and to know what is true, to search for it, as well as to search for who the other person really is.

They say: "What is the use of this? We will know everything after the wedding".

The fiancée may ask her father to accompany her in her engagement, but the father refuses her request and justifies himself by saying: "You will get married soon". In other words, there is a rejection of an analytical view of this relationship for fear that it will end and it is better to close one's eyes and continue on the road to the summit, to the wedding.

The wedding scene is the pinnacle of appearance, not the pinnacle of "logos". In the wedding there is no personal word, but just this sentence: "Yes, I do". The woman as an image is the most distinct thing about the ceremony. Before the wedding, she spends more than six months preparing her outfit. By the time she goes to the church, the bride must be ready, the preparations will last for hours.

When the groom sees her and says, "Is this really you?" she is so disguised, her face is heavily made up, so she becomes an image and not a reality. In the church, the groom stands next to her, he has not put anything on his face and if we want the groom to be beautiful, we try to discipline his hair. During the wedding, we laugh a little, joke a little, and walk around the altar. There is nothing to live for inside and there are no "logos". We repeat the same words at every wedding and even in the wedding ceremony there is no "logos", there are the same words that are always repeated, in this situation where is the "logos"?

Then comes the party and everything that revolves around the chatter. The main question is indeed: "How much will we spend"? People like to party, because they like to be an image and not a reality. We spend a lot of money on the party, to preserve the beautiful image.

When we reach the top of the image, there is not much truth and "logos". When you reach the top of the image, the most dangerous thing afterwards is the fall.

3. The difficulties of dialogue between the wife and the husband

What happens after the wedding?

Some people say, "The situation after the wedding is different from what it was before".

The husband says, "The important thing is that my wife is satisfied with me".

The wife says, "It is important that my husband is satisfied with me and that we listen to each other's wishes".

What is required then after the wedding is that there is mutual consent and that each one knows the needs of the other, it is not necessary to live the truth. But where is the other? And where is his "logos"?

A man can ask his wife to be resourceful, which means that he also wants to do what he wants. This leads to a relationship and a "logos". After the wedding, the images often fall away. The wife discovers a different image of her husband than the one she had of him before and vice versa. The discovery of the other is then made in two different situations, either at home or outside.

We have seen that the fiancée was calm and kind. However, after the wedding, she becomes nervous. As for the fiancé, he was generous and after the wedding he becomes stingy, silent and authoritive at home, but outside he is generous and talkative. We notice a kind of duality; outside the house there are images and inside there is truth; sometimes it is possible that there are images inside the house and truth outside. How do we feel when we find out? How do we feel about each other and ourselves?

We feel disappointment towards the other. You are like that! It is as if each of them has entered a trap; for this reason, the person becomes offensive, aggressive and can generate a spirit of revenge. You let me fall into the trap, so I will show you what I will do! However, these feelings do not leave the house. We feel the sadness of the other or sadness towards the other, that is, a kind of pity. And sometimes we feel the sadness of ourselves, which is an important but at the same time annoying feeling.

The person may feel foolish and cannot easily forgive the other person because he/she thinks that he/she was in a play, that he/she was laughed at, that he/she was cheated. For these reasons, there is a desire for revenge, a difficulty to forgive and there is also a great emptiness. What should I do? And how do I go on?

Some married people say that they cannot stay married, nor love the other. So, a man leaves home, especially if he is financially well off, has kept up activities and relationships, he goes hunting (this does not mean that every man who goes hunting runs away from his wife), he makes society his second home. He cannot stay at home because there is no "logos", no personal word; the image of the other has thus disappeared and the other has lost his image, the truth has become naked. When there is no exchange between two people, there is a kind of boredom, weariness and a kind of death, so what can I do?

The man runs away from home, and the woman quickly gives birth to a second child or a third or a fourth, she takes care of the children. It is a kind of balance so that the marriage can continue. But there are couples who want the truth and refuse to escape. In this case, both parties must have this same desire, so that the marriage can last. Some couples seek the help of a therapist, but I do not think this is necessary unless there are really big problems.

What should I do when I discover that in my relationship with the other (the husband or wife, the fiancé or fiancée, the loved one, the friend, the companion), I am not a "logos", a personal word?

First of all, I desire to become a "logos" for myself, to dialogue with myself. But, how will I become a "logos"? How can I communicate with myself, with my experience and become a word that expresses what I am?

If I do not know myself, I have to talk to myself. If I do not know my fiancé, I have to sit down with him to learn to love him, or just to know him. To know myself, I must take time with myself, I must not run away from myself, nor from the house, nor from my partner. And my decision has to be real and not formal, i.e. I have to go into myself and discover my truth, my personality and who I am. There is a positive isolation here, people who are unable to live with themselves in an intimate relationship will not be able to live it with the other person.

If, in the absence of an intimate relationship with oneself, there is a flight to the outside, the absence of an intimate relationship with the other generates in me the need to escape from him to external relationships, and this may suit some people. The absence of a true relationship with the other is a sign of the absence of a true relationship with oneself, and the absence of positive unity in life.

To know myself, I must learn to be silent and to listen. When I sit with others, I notice that everyone is talking at the same time, i.e. there is not much silence in the conversation, but rather a lull. When one person is silent, another or several other people speak at the same time. There is no subjective second word, i.e. second "logos". Thus, we hear each other and we do not listen to each other. The reason for the absence of listening to each other is the absence of inner silence, why is there no silence?

Indeed, silence allows one or more internal elements to come to the surface; there are those who cannot bear this situation and run away from themselves. Others, faced with silence, live in tension and fear of themselves.

Here I present a small idea of silence based on a simple example:

Let us say I want to walk in nature. Nature is very beautiful in Syria, there is nothing more beautiful than this nature. It is possible that the most beautiful country in the world is Syria. When I walk in nature I see very beautiful things, but most of the time we walk in nature without looking at it, without listening to it, without smelling it, without touching it, i.e. we do not use our senses. The person is used to using reason more than the senses, so many thoughts come to mind and he becomes obsessive. In society there are many obsessives because they think too much. A person could become obsessive if there is not enough connection between his senses and his feelings.

When I walk in nature, I can silence my thoughts in order to listen more. To do this, I have to silence the inner voices by listening to something other than myself, not being locked in myself. When I silence the inner voices by listening to the silence of nature, then a possibility is created to welcome the silence of nature. This is a possible experience and it is not a difficult thing to experience.

Let us look at someone who has a farm, sits down in the night and lights the fire, alone or with a friend or with people who like silence. In this silence, each one feels at ease, he is himself, he does not expect any image of the other and the other also does not expect any image of him. In this situation, I do not expect to give anything to the other, because the other does not expect anything from me. Nobody expects anything from the other, we live in a restful silence. Through this experience, some say that we have felt the silence of harmony; we think that God lives in the silence of harmony. Everyone breathes at their own pace and dialogue is born. Then, when they speak, they can silence their narcissistic voices, their narcissistic thoughts, the ones that go round and round. When I am silent, there is no immediate silence, but there is an external silence, the silence of nature. When I pay attention to nature, I can silence my worries and anxieties, then I listen to the silence and receive it through my stillness, and so my stillness becomes silence.

I always notice that the person who begins to live in silence begins to love himself, so that silence dwells in him, dwells in his body, his person, his whole being. In silence, I love myself in a positive and not negative way; without drawing attention to myself, because I am in a restful silence, in which I want to withdraw to. We experience restful silence when we leave the city of Homs and sit in nature, or when we sit in the chapel of our priest's residence. At nightime or in the church there is a lot of beautiful silence, so I receive the silence and I become silent, and in this silence I listen to my own thoughts. When I say that I love the other person because they think like me, that is not correct, because it does not reveal the uniqueness of the other person. If I think of marrying someone because they think like me and then I notice that they do not feel the way I do, what should I do? I am not like the other person in my feelings and thoughts, no two people feel the same way. If I think that the other person feels the way I feel and loves me the way I love him, we enter into deception here; because feeling is a singular thing.

In my silence, I receive my uniqueness and I listen to my feelings which can be destroyed or rejected, because society does not like my feelings. The education of the person is not to ask for feelings, but rather to ask for a reflection and an image. The feeling removes the image because it is singular, when I feel a feeling, I cannot live in an image because my feeling is singular and real. If I want to be a "logos", a personal word, I have to listen silently to my feelings, but how does this happen? In other words, how can I know myself by listening to my feelings?

We start self-knowledge from childhood, because it is one of the most important stages, so I ask myself: what did I feel in my childhood? Of course, we do not remember everything, but we may have felt jealousy, joy, disappointment, happiness, hatred, revenge, etc. I continue to reread the history of my feelings after the childhood stage, i.e. adolescence and the continuation of adolescence, I reread the wounds that they caused. I reread the feeling I had when people laughed at me and despised me because I did not do well in the baccalaureate, before and after. These are all singular feelings, no one has lived another person's story, so the "I", we notice it in the feelings.

When we reread in silence, the feelings appear and we grasp them. The feelings find a kind of welcoming breast in the silence. When I can really live in silence, I welcome my childhood into the heart of silence, and it is possible for me to feel the negative feelings. I am in a new birth, new feelings emerge, I feel that I am becoming more and more myself.

These feelings, which are in the heart of silence, become a body, and then turn into a speaking body through my words, it is very beautiful. Then, if I remember the history of my feelings, I have become unique, special and personal, then I can talk about my experience. After that I can talk with my fiancé about my experiences during the engagement; the "logos" starts to be in front of me and in me. The person is loved because there is a uniqueness in him, but he is not loved for his idealism, his academic excellence and his lovable image. The person is loved when he is himself, he presents this truth to others, whether they like him or not. But things have become clear, so I can love the other as he is, it is in the realm of feeling. However, there is also the unconscious. The unconscious is the feeling that you have rejected and repressed but which remains buried. If I do not know what is in my unconscious, what can I give myself and the other person of the unconscious?

At the time of the wedding, it appears that there is a great deal of self in the unconscious; I do not know if there will be any big surprises either, because what I did not know before the wedding may appear after the wedding. There may be images and masks that I do not know about. It is possible that a very active person hides laziness in the activity, but does not know it. There is also the person who works a lot for others, he can hide behind this work a feeling of inferiority but he does not know it. The person who appears very strong may be hiding a weakness in his strength. These attitudes are there to compensate, I compensate a lack with its opposite and with things we do not know about ourselves.

It is possible that the unconscious is in the dreams, for example: I am a very calm and peaceful person, yet all my dreams are violent. This means that there is a repressed violence in me that appears in my dreams. Maybe I have discovered this in the analysis of my dreams, but how does this happen?

When I sit in silence and listen to myself, if I look at the dream mentioned before, I ask myself:

is there repressed violence in me? It would be possible to say: at the moment there is no violence. However, this violence comes from my childhood and I have repressed it. This does not mean that the violence in my childhood was always repressed, so the question arises here: if I was violent in my childhood, then I repressed this violence and put on a nice mask so that people would be satisfied with me, because they said: "if you stay like this, we won't like you"? It may be that this is the cause that makes us repress violence and put on a nice mask so that others will like us.

Too often we sacrifice a lot of emotion on the altar of society, so that people will love us, in the way we are asked to. In my dreams I might discover the difference between the conscious and the unconscious. I discover problems between the conscious and the unconscious, they have not met and harmony has not been established between them, I do not know that the unconscious is affecting me. If I were violent in the depth and gentle in the conscious, then it is possible that violence appears, because it cannot remain always in the unconscious.

The unconscious can appear against me through cancer or in some other way. Violence seeks a current and cannot remain repressed in me. Violence can find a river in me against myself.

A girl, for example, can repress her emotions and live on the level of reason, she is excellent at school and everyone congratulates her, but she does not feel much about her body, her emotions, her feelings or her sexuality. What is important to her is her mind, her success and being liked because she is successful in society. This girl does not know that she is repressing her feelings and says: "I am not very emotional". Maybe she sees her dreams as emotional dreams and maybe she does not dream if she represses herself even in her dreams. But what happens at parties, for example?

She sits on her chair without dancing, if she dances, she looks like a piece of wood. She dances a little with one or more boys, but she remains at the level of reason. When she sees another girl, who is spontaneous and simple, then she starts criticizing her, gets angry with her and justifies it by the fact that the girl is frivolous, but she is better than her and she says: "If only all girls were like me"! In other words, she cannot look back at herself and ask: "why am I bothered by this spontaneous girl? What is wrong with me? Why am I not spontaneous"? I think the cause is the reason that organizes, classifies and does not allow the person to be more spontaneous; on top of that, society does not like people to be spontaneous.

Why am I so angry at this girl? If I am angry, there is no problem, but if I am too angry, it indicates that this spontaneous girl reminds me of the spontaneity in me that I do not want to admit; my spontaneity remains repressed. So, in front of the other person's spontaneity, I am afraid of my own spontaneity, my emotions and feelings that I do not want to show either.

When I pay attention to my feelings through my relationship with people, it is possible for me to discover more about my unconscious. If I despise myself in people, then I despise myself in despising them. What I despise in people may be in myself, I may have repressed it because I reject it. If I want to know more about my unconscious, I have to pay attention to the feelings I have in my daily life, in my relationships with others and ask myself: "why do I get angry"?

In general, the active person gets angry at the lazy person, it is possible that the laziness is repressed in him. So, I analyse little by little, according to my feelings, where I exaggerate in my relationship with others. If we give a person the opportunity to listen to their conscious story, they indirectly explore their unconscious story. So when a man talks to his wife, he will have more than an image, he will have a "logos", a personal word, so the "logos" begins to talk about itself, silently listens to his experience, as he silently listens to his wife's experience, if she too has taken this step to know herself. If she does not take this step, it will be a big problem in the couple. For us to live a true marriage, both parties must each become a "logos", a personal word, and when each of them accepts to talk about themselves in an atmosphere of listening, it becomes a zone of love between them, that is to say a "dia". There is no love if there are not two "logos", two personal words and a "dia".

Then comes the opportunity to ask an important question: am I allowed to have a child if I am not a "logos"? Is it permissible to have a child if both parents are not "logos" and if there is no "dia"?

When each of the parents is not a singular word and there is no field between them for listening and love, the child becomes mute despite learning to speak. If the child is not born of dialogue, it will become mute later. In other words, if the child is not born in an atmosphere of love, it cannot later become a true "logos", because in love the person is discovered and born, and in the absence of love the self does not exist, it is absent. Love allows the self and the word to appear in the child. Love calls the child by desiring from it a singular word. Love does not demand submission to the words of others. In love, I desire to listen to the other, to listen to the child so that it becomes a "logos", a word.

The father and the mother, when they listen to each other out of love in front of the child, the child becomes a word, because the "logos" is born where there is the "dia". We create this field of love when we listen to the other, so the other becomes more and more a "logos", a word. In marriage, when the person becomes more and more a "logos", he or she lives more and more in silence. In the love relationship, there is a possibility to receive the child who, thanks to love and listening, will be able to become a word for himself and a word to dialogue with the other. When in marriage there is no "logos" and dialogue, it is necessary that marriage becomes a workshop to achieve "logos" and dialogue. However, it is not desirable for a married couple to have a child before having "logos" and dialogue, otherwise the child is born in the ditch.

III. FROM THE MASK
TO THE TRUTH

The beauty of nature is that it wears no mask, because everything is natural in it. When we see a tree, for example, we notice that it grows naturally from its roots and grows in harmony with this stump that has imposed itself and gradually emerges. When the tree grows, it grows from within, no one can impose on the tree, by force, what is not there in it from the beginning. In other words, there is dynamic growth, and Mark's Gospel speaks of the kingdom of God: "26 This is what the kingdom of God is like: someone casts seed in his field. 27 Night and day, whether he sleeps or rises, the seed sprouts and grows without his knowing how. 28 The earth makes the stalk of the plants grow of its own accord, and then the ear, and finally plenty of wheat in the ear. 29 When the wheat is ripe, they go to work with the sickle, for the time of harvest has come" (Mk 4:26-29).

After reading this text, we realize that no one can hide an element of nature. He must provide the conditions for the growth of the tree or the wheat by using fertilizer, providing the plowing and watering without affecting the origin of the tree and then sleep without doing anything else. In nature there is a dynamic growth that starts from the origin, which gives each tree its uniqueness, because no two trees are the same, just as no two branches or leaves are the same. In the spring, the uniqueness of each tree is revealed in the way it grows, in its branches, its leaves and its shape.

What happens in nature also happens in man. When we talk about the life of God in man according to the text of Mark, the person who wants to grow dynamically and who wants God to live in him, must sleep without affecting the presence of God in him, he lets God act in him, without putting a mask on the face of God; this is how the work of God will appear in him automatically. It is necessary for us to receive the Spirit of God so that God lives in us by His Spirit and God can appear in us with His Spirit by promoting the conditions of growth.

Every human being is a force-driven being, which means that everything that exists in him will also be realized in action in one way or another; education plays an important role here between the exercise of this force and the role of action. The fetus is born without a mask, the educator must raise the child who possesses something intrinsically innate and this education passes through the stages of childhood, adolescence and maturity. Man did not create these stages because they are attached to his origin. The educator is not the one who makes the child go through these stages, however, he must provide the conditions so that the child can go through them naturally from the beginning. The educator gives something to the child and does not expect everything to become obvious or innate in the child, because there are innate and acquired elements in the child. The art of education is to present to the child something acquired which could help him reach personal fulfillment that it harmonizes with what is in him, without stifling what is innately present in him from the beginning. Thus, the child can always express his innate origin with what he has acquired.

The problem with us is education, because we do not allow the child to build himself from what exists in him, we should indeed listen to him to know what exists in him and let it manifest itself, develop. When the child is born, we make him wear masks as soon as possible, we put our masks on this innocent child or we wish it to be so. We do not listen to him because we do not assume that there is anything innate in the child as there is in the tree. Man cannot put his masks on the tree, but he can put his masks on the little child from birth, or be persuaded to put them on.

There is a beautiful German film called "The Drum". In this film, a child is born, he is very young when he appears in this film and he has heard what he is told. He looks at his surroundings as if he were an adult, but what does he hear when he comes out of his mother's womb?

He hears his mother say: "I do not want my son to be as quarrelsome as my husband. I want him to be polite, reasonable and kind like my father, but not like my husband". But sometimes the mother wants the child to become like his own father. So from the beginning, a mask is put on the newborn. So, in education, sometimes we stick something to the child that comes from our parents, from our friends, from those we love or from God.

The father says: "I do not want a reasonable, polite, nice boy, but rather a strong boy to take over the store from me. He must be shrewd in this world, or he will not be able to live, he must fight in this life to learn". What the father asks for is the opposite of what the mother wants, so there are two different images. The problem with the masks is that from the beginning there are two masks, one mask that the mother proposes and another that the father suggests, and then these two masks struggle inside the boy, because the boy wants to be both as his mother wishes and as his father wishes.

The boy noticed the contradiction of this life, he saw that there was no fidelity between the spouses, each one tries to appear sincere, but it is not the truth. The boy thus decides not to grow up, but rather to remain small, without a mask, not to become as his mother wishes, nor as his father wishes, but rather to be as he wants. He holds a drum and plays the drum as he walks through the streets in rebellion against this masked society.

We understand through this film that there are people like this boy, they are small and then grow up. They have to represent the image of the mother, against the image of the father or vice versa, or they have to try to be both at the same time, but they do not succeed. There are people who try to be themselves and succeed if there is no pressure on them.

When the fetus is born, it does not have a mask, but very quickly one is put on it, it cannot free itself from it because the mask has merged with its personality since its birth.

Let us take a look at another film: "Autumn Sonata". In this film we see Eva receiving her mother after a long absence of seven years. We see Eva with her hair up, her glasses like a little girl's and her face is emaciated and yellow, like the face of a dead person. Eva's life is empty and joyless. She has a kind of sweetness but she is cold; Eva is a very polite girl, but she has no personality, her face is not expressive. She wonders when she can take off her mask.

Maybe when someone likes her as she is, without asking her to hide. She hides because she thinks that if she appears in her truth, people will laugh at her and despise her. Eva's mother did not like her, so she recreated another image of Eva in her dreams that she liked.

Eva said to her mother: "You didn't like anything about my life, I was insignificant in front of you, I felt that I had nothing for myself and I was afraid that you would reject me. So I started to tell myself that I would have to do everything you asked me to do so that you wouldn't be angry with me. I became a toy in your hands, you played with me as you wanted. I began to speak as you spoke, to wear your clothes and to imitate your movements I entered completely in the image that you desired of me. I became a faceless mask, I became dead behind your image, plastered on my face. My face suggests death because I am not yet born, I am born in the flesh, but as a person I am not yet born".

During the conversation Eva had with her mother, she realized that her face did not reflect her personality because she was wearing a mask. She thus began to gradually free herself from the hatred she felt towards her mother, the cause of her mask, and also to free herself from the repression she had experienced.

Through these two films, we have approached two types of masks. However, not all masks are the same, because I can put a mask on my face after having experienced painful events that have caused a great wound in my heart. I then want to hide this wound with a mask so that people do not see it, so that they do not reject me or laugh at me.

I will now give two more examples. The first one is about exposure to a sexual incident and the second one is about a young man named Amer, who loved a girl named Tamara.

In the first example, a young girl, Najat, was exposed to sexual abuse in her family, and then she hated sex, men, emotions, and the body. She gradually distanced herself from all these subjects.

It is important to know that when a person moves away from essential subjects such as emotions, feelings, emotional and sexual life and the body, the color of his face changes. Previously, the smile was on his face and it revealed the life in him, but when the person refuses what warms the heart, such as emotions, then his face becomes yellow and lifeless. What happens in such a situation?

Najat, because of her wounds, turns away from her emotions, her sex life, her body and turns to reason, to will. She works hard to develop her reason and her will. She succeeds in school, in university. She becomes a brilliant mind, superior to the professors who accompanied her in her studies. She begins to show her superiority over the male scholars. Najat has put on her face and her emotional wounds a rigid scientific mask through which she fights others.

In the second example, it is Amer who loved Tamara. Amer liked the image in Tamara that he liked to see in the woman. We call this type of image, the joint image, for the man or for the woman. Amer liked the image of his spouse in Tamara, and Tamara at first felt that Amer liked her very much. However, because Amer liked the image of his partner in Tamara, he tried to possess Tamara and observe her because he was jealous of her and did not want to lose his image of the woman in Tamara. In the end, Tamara begins to be bothered by the way Amer treats her, she realizes that if Amer continues to be jealous, possessive and controlling, she will leave him. However, Amer did not pay attention to his behavior, and the result was that Tamara left him. Amer then felt rejected and experienced aggressive feelings towards Tamara.

When we feel aggression in our lives, saying that it is caused by betrayal and because we are oppressed, then aggression turns into sadness. Because I am rejected, abandoned and oppressed, I become a victim. When I become sad, oppressed and a victim, I try to attract the eyes of others to me so that they see that I am a victim, I then ask for their compassion. I put on my aggressiveness the mask of sadness and then over that a mask of humour because people may not show pity when they see someone sad and weak, they will want someone else. Bitter says: "Why should I stay sad? I will be funny, because if I joke, my friends will like me". Humour shows a kind of strength. Thus, Amer put a mask of sadness on his aggressiveness, then a mask of humor on his sadness.

In these two examples, we see that the person puts a mask on his face after a certain injury, in order to hide the fact that he has been hurt. The question is: can we take off the mask we have put on or not? It is not easy, because for such a long time I have been joking around, or some time ago I was a victim of sexual abuse, and then I became mentally rigid, voluntarily intelligent and educated, and this for such a long time. We cannot ask Najat to lift the mask or Amer not to joke, because it is not such an easy thing.

I will mention now, other masks that I can wear and remove frequently, among them: makeup.

- A woman can put different types of makeup on her face, red, green, etc. Does what is used for beauty become a mask?

It is not a mask as long as it does not stifle what is natural, but rather preserves what is naturally beautiful and highlights it. As long as I do not overdo the amount of makeup applied, exaggerating the black, green and purple colors. The mask hides the expression of what is inside.

The mask can also be a perfume. If the perfume is pleasant, it can express without exaggeration the beauty of the interior. But when I overuse perfume to the point of preventing those around me from doing yoga exercises, or to the point of perfuming the whole neighborhood, then it becomes a kind of mask and we know that this action is not right.

- The diplomat is obliged to wear a mask when he welcomes people. He must smile and this mask is required of him. It is not normal for an ambassador to welcome his guests crying, only because he feels like crying. Smiling in this situation is a good mask and then when he gets home he can cry on his wife's shoulder for as long as he pleases and then live out what he feels.

- Someone appears outside the house helpful, good, generous and kind, but at home he seems stingy, useless, selfish and cruel. It should not be said, however, that he wears a mask outside and does not wear it inside. It is possible that there is no mask either outside the house or inside; this man is helpful, generous and at the same time he is stingy.

Sometimes we cannot tell if there is a mask or not. There are masks that are printed on my face to the point that my face has become a mask and the mask has become a part of my face. For this reason, it is difficult to remove the mask because I have to remove my face at the same time.

However, when I discover masks in my life, how do I move from the masks to the truth of myself? What should I do?

Firstly, you have to acknowledge that there are masks, and then remove them. But how does this happen?

We see in the Bible that Peter wore the mask of strength, but when did Peter become aware of this mask? When he denied Christ, his weakness was discovered and the mask of strength fell off. Accidents in life can help us discover the truth about ourselves. For example, if a person always feels anxious in the presence of others, it indicates that he or she is hiding something and that there are masks that hide his or her true personality.

Others, such as a husband or wife or children, may draw my attention to the presence of a mask, or I discover it for myself through reading and my relationship with God. I think God is the one who feels my masks the most, why? When I get to know God through a personal relationship and not through ideas, I am aware that God is the True One and the Truth, that He does not lie and that He is good. When I am in front of a very pure person, I feel impure, and so the more pure the person in front of me is, the less pure I feel, so I discover my masks.

Can I remove all the masks I put on my face? I think that it is not possible to remove all of them, because one does not know all of one's masks and there is a crossover between masks and personality. Suppose someone says that joking, strength, insults, weakness etc. are masks, he cannot remove them all. He may discover that behind the mask of his strength is weakness; if he wants to remove the mask of strength, he will appear weak and people will laugh at him. It is better to keep some masks and have pity on ourselves, provided that we free ourselves from what is behind the masks.

If there is a mask of weakness behind strength, I work to find out where that weakness comes from and I become stronger. And if I joke a lot to hide my sadness, I work to discover the cause of my sadness, then I joke not to hide my sadness, but out of a desire to joke. In this way, joking does not remain a mask, but rather becomes an expression of the state of joy and pleasure in which I live. Knowing what is behind the mask requires a kind of analysis, truth and introspection.

In the film "Autumn Sonata", Eva expresses all the hatred she feels towards her mother. Then, little by little, her face changes, she takes off her glasses and releases her hair onto her shoulders, then her eyes express the violence she is carrying. Thus, from the confrontation and the expression of what has been repressed, life begins to flow and it emerges, from the hatred that was behind her face, with tenderness and forgiveness.

The one who expresses tenderness is an authentic person who does not wear a mask. Eva realizes that she has harmed her mother with her old hatred. So, after being freed from this hatred, her true face is revealed and, after her mother leaves, Eva writes her a letter, saying: "I have wronged you and tormented you because of my old hatred, so I ask for your forgiveness".

In our lives, there is grace and opportunity to care for one another, to help one another, and to live out tenderness together. When I can forgive a person, I am reborn, and when I forgive with all my heart, I am freed from my masks. But sometimes, because I cannot forgive the other person, I put the mask of hardness on my tenderness, and because I do not want to discover the hardness in me or acknowledge it, my heart becomes hard.

When Amer realized that there was sadness behind the joke and aggression behind the sadness, he had begun to express that aggression through his words and he was no longer sad. Then he admitted that he was being unfair to Tamara. When he discovered that he was the oppressor, perhaps he put on the mask of justification to hide his unfairness? Amer wanted to seek the truth of himself, he asked himself: "why am I an oppressor? Why do I want from Tamara what I do not have? Why do I not realize these things myself instead of asking Tamara to embody my image of a woman?"

Amer was a businessman, he didn't have time to read, to do art, to receive people and listen to them. He wanted Tamara to realize what she was missing. If Amer wanted to free himself from the mask of work that his emotions and his image of a woman hid behind, he had to become himself again and live listening, doing art, receiving people and reading, living close to nature and the earth, devoting time to all of thes.

Amer began to take an interest in art, to draw and write, and then he saw his companion come back to life in him. Now he can see the woman for what she is and not a reflection of his image of her or his need for her. Thus, he could listen to the woman as a woman and discover her own nature through strength and action. Thus, he feels free.

If Amer is able to listen to and feel Tamara, then this new relationship will allow them to make a new start, each of them being able to offer something to the other without one trying to realize his image through the other and vice versa.

Peter felt ashamed by his denial of Christ. He thought he was very strong and different from others who were weak. He discovered his weakness in his denial of Christ. Indeed, he denied Christ because he felt that Christ was becoming weak and Peter was looking for a strong person to feel through him that he was strong. His mask fell off and he did not become a subject of mockery by people because Christ was at his side and looked at him with a look of love. Peter accepted his weakness and discovered his true strength when he felt that Christ loved him.

When someone accepts his weakness, he does not need artificial strength to cover his weakness and he can discover his real strength. This means that strength is real, but sometimes it is a mask depending on whether one accepts one's weakness or not.

In Najat's example, we see that she ran away from abuse as a child, she does not want to remember the sexual assault anymore. So what is the solution in this case? Her face is yellow and rigid, lifeless and hopeless, reflecting only will and reason. She needs to go back to these repressed events, to know what she is really experiencing and to realize that her superiority over the male scholars is a mask, that she is taking revenge on them.

If she asks: "why am I getting back at them?" She can remember the repressed event in the unconscious, either from dreams or during a conversation. This discovery causes great pain and a great cry. When someone has a tooth pulled out, a great cry of pain comes out with it. When Najat agrees to think about what happened with the pain of the discovery, the pain of a new birth, she can overcome these steps despite the pain.

It is important that she remembers the incident

well, closing her eyes and remembering everything and all the details again. Remembering and experiencing the event allows one to live the feelings associated with the experience and the image, in order to free oneself from this image.

We return to the example of Amer who thought he had been wronged but recognized that he was unfair. It is possible that Najat can say that she is a little unfair to men and not just oppressed. She then begins to open up to life again. In this case, the color of her face changes as the color of Eva's face has changed. Then the warmth returns, a new dawn begins, she passes from the face of death to the face of life.

From these examples, we have tried to explain that the important thing is not to remove the masks, but rather to remove what is behind them so that the person becomes more serene and real.

Seeing what is behind the masks does not mean that the masks do not exist. The person needs to meet themselves more, by taking time to be alone, to discover what is positive in them and to find a solution to a specific problem, so that they can become more authentic in front of people.

When masks are printed on our faces, we will not be able to remove them. If there is a bright sun within us, the person discovers the light that melts these masks little by little. Thus, the sunlight that comes out from within and shines on the masks creates a kind of illumination. So the masks that are attached to my face remain, but they become my true face.

IV. THE INTERPRETATION OF DREAMS ACCORDING TO FREUD

Freud was born in Austria in 1856 and died in 1939 in London. He was the first psychoanalyst and the founder of psychoanalysis.

We will talk about the function of dreams according to Freud and the free association of ideas that Freud uses to discover the meaning of a dream.

The function of the dream according to Freud

The function of the dream according to Freud is to realize conscious and unconscious desires.

1. The fulfillment of conscious desires in the dream

Firstly, I'll talk about the "I". It is possible that "I" exists more in the eyes of people, so what is "I"? Is "I" the way people see me? Or how I want people to see me through the image I present to them?

Sometimes the problem is that I see myself based on how people see me, like a daughter who looks at herself negatively through her mother's negative view of her.

I want to see myself without relying on people's view of the particular "I", by isolating myself from people for a bit, listening to myself and asking myself: who am I without people's view of me? To answer this question, I have to remain relaxed, and silent for a little while to try and feel who I am. Usually there is a difficulty when we ask someone to relax and feel without seeing people.

It is important that I rest in front of the other person without taking into account his look on me. However, it is difficult to rest at ease in front of the other, because I always take into account his look, as if I were in front of a professor or a teacher or in front of a judge in a courtroom. There is a desire to succeed in this relationship, but there is the fear of the failure of this relationship, the fear that the other does not like me, for that reason, I am not natural in front of him.

When I listen to myself, I ask myself: what do I feel? There are people who only feel emptiness. Because to know the "I", you have to isolate yourself from people. I can meet myself in silence by closing my eyes and listening to myself. When the "I" does not appear as "I", in this case there is emptiness. There are people who say that they feel a lack, an existential lack, because "I can feel that I am not present as I am, and I can also feel a lack of confidence". There are other people who say that you feel beauty, the "I" is beautiful, but "I do not feel it much because I am always surrounded by people". There are also other people who say that there is the social "I", the psychological "I", and the spiritual "I" in them. The spiritual "I" is the one who loves and seeks creativity. The one who loves is dynamic, he opens himself up to life and throws himself into its space. The spiritual "I" is the one who appreciates beauty and loves others and their beauty. There is the fourth "I", that is the "I" of the unconscious, which means that there is a part of the unconscious in me, I do not know it and I do not feel it. How can I recognize it if I do not know it and if I do not feel it? Freud proposes to analyze dreams. Freud was the first to carry out a scientific analysis of a dream, starting from the person who dreams about his conscious and unconscious life.

There was an interpretation of dreams before Freud, but it was not based on the unconscious of the dreamer. We find it in the Old Testament or in other books, a great character saw a dream, then his dream was interpreted in the framework of a group, that is to say that this dream does not concern only this great character, but rather his people and his future.

It has been reported that God speaks directly in the dream, while Freud said that it is the unconscious or the conscious that speaks, it is not

God who speaks directly. About this idea, I have two remarks to make:

The first remark is that Freud does not say that in the dream there is only the unconscious, but he says that there is conscious and unconscious desires that are clearly realized in the dream. To clarify this point, I will cite some examples.

In my conscious life, I have a desire to eat chocolate and then I dream that I am eating chocolate, so in my dream a conscious desire appears and is realized there. Here, there is no unconscious, but a concrete consciousness about my daily life. There are different dreams of this kind, for example, when a person lives alone all the time and is tormented by isolation, he or she may dream that he or she is at a party with people and dancing. This dream compensates through the imagination for a conscious lack that was felt during the day. Another example is someone who is afraid to undergo a surgical procedure and sees in his or her dream that the operation was successful. This person has wished during the day that the operation would be successful, so they see in their dream that their wish has been granted and feel safe in the dream because the operation was successful. Another example is someone who lives in Canada and wants to return to Syria. However, he is reluctant to go back even though his desire is greater than staying in Canada. He wants to go back, but he is afraid that his children will not come back with him; they may tell him that they will stay in Canada. He tries to convince them by saying that he has a factory in Homs, money, a house, friends and a neighborhood that he belongs to, and that he really wants to back.go. Maybe he thinks his children will convince him to stay in Canada, so what does he dream about? He dreams that he is getting ready for the trip, opening the closet, taking some clothes and leaving others. He feels safe because he wants to return, and this wish comes true in his dream. The primary function of dreams for Freud is the fulfillment of conscious desires that are subject to deprivation and in the dream we compensate for this lack.

The second remark is that people ask themselves: why do we deal with the unconscious? Why do we walk on this royal path of the unconscious to discover it? The unconscious causes problems, so without it it is better, so I stay in the conscious and I am happy because, through the unconscious, I will discover repressed desires and things that are not good, I'd better live without them. However, it seems to me that it is very important to discover the unconscious through dreams. I will give three simple examples among many others.

The first example: a mother who spoils her child too much and loves him excessively. It is possible that she is experiencing violence in the unconscious towards this child, so she compensates for the violence with an excessive increase in kindness. The mother must know that there is violence in the unconscious towards her child, and by spoiling him too much, she represses this feeling. But one wonders: why should she be aware of this? Because the child feels the unconscious, we do not raise the child only with the conscious, but we raise it more with the unconscious.

Second example: a girl is looking for the image of her father in the future husband, and after the marriage she wants to see the image of her father only in her husband, and because of this she suffers a lot. The husband feels that his wife does not love him for his personality, but rather that she loves the image of her father in him. This situation leads to many problems.

Third example: a young man prefers to find a young girl who is quiet, polite, shy and without much life experience. After marriage, she cannot live freely because her husband tries to possess her. So she sees violent dreams, people shooting at each other, they are angry and nervous. She does not know the meaning of her dreams, although a large part of her personality is in her dreams and not in her conscious life.

Many surprises happen to newlyweds, because their image of the other was not what they thought. As for those who have been married for many years, because they have gone through painful experiences, it is possible that the truth appears to them and they discover the unconscious and the conscious in new elements of each other's personality.

2. The fulfillment of unconscious desires in the dream

I first talk about the dream as a physical-physiological phenomenon. In 1950, scientists conducted a study on the person who dreams and the physical symptoms that accompany the person during a dream. They discovered, through the use of electronic machines, that an adult person dreams at least four times during the night. When a person dreams, physical symptoms appear: the eyebrows start to tremble, the heart beats rapidly and breathing accelerates. The dream is prolonged according to the four stages of the dream, in the fourth stage, the dream can last an hour.

They found that a forty-year-old woman was dreaming of walking down a popular street with a large suitcase. Suddenly, the suitcase opens and her underwear comes out, she feels very uncomfortable and begins to gather these items and close the suitcase. But she cannot gather all the items because some of them remain on the sidewalk. The lady in her dream sees that people look at her things and laugh in mockery.

The woman is bourgeois and does not like the popular street, because she thinks that these people from the popular street directly discover the other in her and feel it. She does not like that the other feels her and discovers her. When the suitcase opens, which symbolizes her, her personal things come out, so she feels ashamed. This is the interpretation of this dream. This lady does not like herself, she is ashamed of herself. She escapes from people so that they do not find out what she is like. However, the suitcase opened in the street and everything came out publicly, despite her attempt to pick up the clothes. She wanted to be like a closed suitcase, but the clothes stayed out, which made people laugh.

Through free association of ideas, it is possible to enter more into the life of this woman to see the childhood or other problems that make her see this dream. Freud says that the dream is the royal path to the unconscious. We have seen that it is very important to discover one's unconscious, because the unconscious can negatively affect my life and my choices. Through dreams, I can get to know my problems.

Is it a good thing that problems reveal themselves?

For example, a girl thinks she has a reserved femininity, so she always wears pants. After discovering that she has a problem with her femininity, is this discovery good? Of course, because now she can face the problem. As long as the problem is unconscious, she cannot face it. We must not forget that the repressed, rejected unconscious will come out whether we want it to or not. The repressed unconscious may come out in dreams, nervousness or sensitivity. If you continue to live the repression, you become more sensitive, more nervous and more violent.

In the first step, the unconscious must become conscious. And the second step, it has to come out, through boxing or some other activity.

It is possible that sex appears consciously as feelings and when I learn that I am a sexual person and that sex is in me, I cannot reject it. Sex is indirectly in all things, in prayer, friendship, drawing, etc. It is not in one specific place. The person who expresses himself in several areas has a serene sexual life. As for the person who cannot express his humanity and does not have a correct relationship with himself, with the other and with God, he does not feel comfortable in his sexual life, even if he has sexual relations, because what is repressed in him has not been expressed. It is necessary to know how I can be a full human being. In other words, I need to know how I can be more artistic, more helpful, etc., so that this energy comes out with a purpose and I can relax.

A person may become aware of strong feelings of violence towards their mother or father, and those who are still alive. What can I do with violent feelings? Do I tell my kind, elderly father that he was abusive? How should I express what is inside me towards my father without treating him harshly or saying a hurtful word? The subject needs wisdom and we do not want to harm the other person, consciously or unconsciously. So I only tell him unconsciously: I have discovered my violence towards you and now I want to express this violence, I will show you what I could not show you when I was a child because you were strong and I was weak, but now I am stronger than you. This method does not carry any love. I have to express in another way what is inside me and know that the repressed violence has come out of me. When the repressed violence comes out, what follows is tenderness. Sadness hides violence and violence hides tenderness in general. It is better that the person is violent than sad, it is better that he is affectionate than violent.

In myself, there are several levels. If I want to go further and discover different feelings in order to reach deep and positive emotions, I become more affectionate with my parents, who were not nice to me in my childhood.

We can say that discovering the unconscious is important because the more I discover the unconscious, the more sincere I become with myself, with the other, with God, and with all those who love the truth. If I want to reach more truth, I have to work on myself and confront my reality.

There are people who do not want confrontation or access to the truth, there are others who like to reach the truth and enter into the adventure of confrontation. And you, what would you choose?

V. HOW DO WE LIVE WITH FEAR AND ANXIETY?

What are fear and anxiety? What are their causes and varieties?

Fear is an emotional reaction to a danger, whether it comes from outside of man or from within. Fear is manifested by physical phenomena, such as a lack of hearing, shortness of breath, increased heart rate or shaking of the hands and feet and other signs.

Anxiety is a disturbed psychological state that occurs in anticipation of danger, without the cause of the danger being known.

What we repress, we project onto society, like "the evil eye". When we have repressed violence, for example, we project this violence onto others through what we call "the evil eye". People are afraid of the eye because they have a lot of violence in them. It works as if a person has feelings of envy, they try to project them onto others.

We are afraid of a lot of things, I'll name a few fears:

1. Fear of losing. We are afraid of illness, of old age. We are also afraid of losing our dignity,

of losing the positive image that we give of ourselves, of losing our fortune, our position and power.

2. The fear of a person. Indeed, when he rejects me, he becomes hostile, he shows his violence towards me and tries to take revenge.

3. Fear of myself, my weaknesses, my failures, or fear of repressed instinctive feelings. Fear of the dark, the street, the elevator, animals, etc.

4. Fear of the future, because it is unknown to us. We remove this fear of the future by showing strength in order to face it in a positive way. We remove the unknown side inherent in the future by succeeding in our studies, by learning a language or a trade.

We can say that the sources of fear are divided between innate and acquired sources.

1. Innate fear: associated with human nature. Fear is genetically transmitted in some cases. The fetus receives its mother's anxiety through breastfeeding

2. Acquired fear: it manifests itself when we ask something of the child and make him/her fear that we will not love him/her if he/she does not do it. The child believes our words, so we plant negative thoughts in the child's mind instead of positive ones.

We ask: How can we live with fear and anxiety?

Most of us live with fear and anxiety by running away. But we can live with fear and anxiety through a psychological re-reading of fear and anxiety, and then dive deep within ourselves to learn about its causes and consequences. For the child who is afraid of the street, for example, by analyzing this fear, we conclude that it goes back far beyond the fear of the street, because it can be linked to the fear of the horse. And when we continue the research on the source of this fear, we can see that it was his father who instilled it in him. In this way, we get to know the cause of his fear, without dwelling on the primitive elements on which the fear was projected.

I will present another example: a young girl is beautiful and intelligent, she is successful in her studies and her work. But she is anxious and fears failure in her new relationships with young people. She is advanced in age and no young man has proposed to her. In the end, she meets someone older than her, who is of a lower social class than her and has no education. She begins to experience a kind of confusion, either to refuse him or to accept him. In order for this girl to find a solution to her problem, she needs to take time to think about it.

Generally, the person is afraid of his repressed feelings and there is a conflict between him and what has been repressed in him. Can we identify what is repressed in us? Do I have the courage to reread my life story to explain the frightening incidents, then free myself from what scares me and learn to live again?

If this young girl rereads her past, she will discover that she has been spoiled by her younger sisters and parents, but her older sisters are jealous and project negative thoughts onto her that do not exist within her. This young girl has subconsciously repressed the fact that her older sisters do not love her. When she grew up, she felt that she was not beautiful and she unconsciously repressed her feelings to show a beautiful image of herself. She repressed in the unconscious part of the ugly girl personality that her sisters projected on her. The unconscious began to provide her with destructive thoughts, such as not being worthy of someone. When this girl enters her unconscious, she will feel sorry for the little girl inside her and she will care more for herself.

I would say that through the memory, the person is moving from a mental discovery to a mental acceptance, and is thus moving out of her painful past and seeking to live in the present. If this girl has moved from the repressed past to the conscious and has realized what is repressed in her, then she will discover what is in her being, receive from herself what is precious and share it with others.

I could do this rereading of my past alone, or I

could ask someone to help me. In both cases, we come to terms with what is repressed in us and experience a new birth by putting aside the primitive elements on which we have projected fear and look for the root cause.

When this girl allows the little girl in her to grow and the big girl in her to become smaller, a new birth will occur.

VI. INNER PEACE

Is it what we experienced in the past that we are not experiencing in the present? Is it the lost paradise? Is this what we will experience later? Or is it what we will experience only in another life after death?

There are several reasons why we ask these questions, among them:

- The evolution of our time, which is difficult for us to follow because this evolution is fast and is imposed on us from outside. Because of it, we feel a kind of loss!

- The ignorance of the future, which is unknown and ambiguous.

- The absence of a solid basis on which to build our present and our future.

- The anxiety that accompanies the process of rapid development.

- Increased living expenses and decreased income.

- Marital problems.

- The problems between parents and children.

- The emigration of young people and the increase in the number of single girls.

We ask the question: was it difficult for those who lived before us, about fifty or a hundred years ago, to acquire inner peace? Religion and faith played an important role in people's lives. Faith sought to unite people, to give meaning to life and to create a kind of inner peace. Moreover, religious practices require effort, they are an ongoing spiritual journey and struggle. However, some people say: "I want to reach inner peace by myself and I will isolate myself to search for it". However, trying to find inner peace alone is difficult. The method of achieving inner peace lies in the liberation from all forms of bondage. This liberation is difficult.

For example, migrating to a new country is difficult, because the individual has received a value from his society of which he has a thorough knowledge, but no one knows him in the new society. The same is true when a person undertakes a journey to his inner world. Leaving one reality to go to another is not an easy thing, like the exodus of the Jewish people from Egypt, from the land of slavery to the promised land. The man will first arrive in an isolated area where there is no one and, perhaps, the new reality will generate a feeling of boredom.

When I seek to be alone with myself, it is not necessary to come directly to the meeting, there are means to help us to introspect, such as music, reading or the practice of a hobby. After having achieved mental isolation, man will wait for the spring when the earth puts on its new green dress. When a person listens to himself in all sincerity, he will make emerge from his unconscious what has been repressed, has made him live in anguish and has deprived him of inner peace.

In order to live in silence, there must be a silent setting or environment that helps the person to remain silent and to listen to themselves so that they can contemplate themselves as they meditate on the Bible. The group plays a positive role in observing silence and listening to oneself, as does nature.

When the person is listening to himself, he may not accept himself because now he knows himself better, but he has to die, in a way, that is to say, to reject the scars that are in himself in order to arrive at inner peace. There is, therefore, a time when the person lives the death of the scars by freeing himself from what is repressed, then he lives a period of mourning, before accepting himself.

Running away from the confrontation with oneself produces a feeling of guilt or a feeling of inferiority or even a feeling of self-punishment, sacrificing oneself in one form or another without being aware of it. However, accepting a certain death is an important step towards achieving inner peace. Overcoming the fear of the death of scars is much more difficult than accepting death itself. If a person knows what is preventing them from experiencing inner peace, they will achieve it. If the person does not overcome the death of scars and the fear of death, he will continue to cry over himself, over his loss. But the one who believes that God is love and mercy will not cry for long.

I would like to tell a true story here. There was a woman, a university doctor, well known, who did not know inner peace. She discovered through silence and listening that there were two characters within her. The first character was that of a shy and intelligent teenager, whom she rejects and hates. The second was that of a mature and successful doctor. But, for this doctor to come to terms with her psychological history, these two characters must meet within her.

Generally speaking, the person must face his or her problems, such as failure in love or studies, and forgive himself or herself. Indeed, the inability to forgive oneself does not lead to inner peace, and reconciliation with one's psychological history does not necessarily mean that one achieves inner peace! It is possible that the person feels a certain psychological comfort after a session of psychoanalysis or silence experienced with a companion, but what is experienced here is not inner peace. It is necessary to follow the path within oneself, believing that God's goodness is present in the depths of our being. When the person frees himself from what is repressed in him, he can find comfort and the silence will be easy to live. Thus, when the person reaches reconciliation with himself, he can listen to the divine dimension that is present in him, while knowing that this divine dimension cannot be grasped. Rather, the person must wait patiently for this divine transfiguration and when this transfiguration is experienced, he or she will live the spring. One should not get bored or despair or give up the process, but rather follow the path until one reaches the light!

There are two ways to live this encounter with the light. The first is to live fully with a feeling of great joy, of deep inner peace and this may be accompanied by tears. The second is to live in a gentle way by practicing continuous silence. In this way, the person will arrive at inner peace, joy and consolation.

Everything in life requires effort and time, the person must live the silence gradually, living it day by day, perhaps starting with a quarter of an hour a day, then a half hour, and so on. With practice, silence will become an integral part of human life. In inner silence and inner peace, the person overcomes difficult experiences and distances himself from his daily difficulties. Problems will weigh less on the person, because he or she has a solid internal basis that carries these problems.

When the person lives in peace, he or she feels that his or her peace positively affects his or her relationship with others. When the person can discover the spirit of God present in himself, he will surely be able to discover the spirit of God present in others. If the person does not discover the spirit of God in him as a gift of God, he will not discover the other gifts of God. True inner peace is discovering the Spirit of God in everything.

In the end, if the inner peace I have discovered in myself is deep, it will remain. It takes patience and listening to discover that God is in every person and in everything around us. Inner peace is discovering that God is in everything.

CONCLUSION

The themes that Father Frans addresses to the woman and the man of today help to discover personal values, to accept the other and to discover the good in him.

Fr. Frans shows that through silence and nature, alone or with a group, man can listen to himself and discover with time the light in himself, in others and in all things.

Father Frans sought through psychoanalysis to deepen self-knowledge so that man could discover himself and learn to know himself better.

Through his conferences, Father Frans offers the means for each person to analyze and deepen his or her inner life and to have a clearer answer to the question: Who am I?

In the second volume, we will deal with other conferences on self-love, love of the other, self-esteem, marital relationships and other topics.

BIBLIOGRAPHY

Three lectures are transcribed word for word in Arabic dialect by Caroline AL-RAHEB: "Why I like to live and why I don't like to live", "The difficulty of dialoguing with oneself and with the other" and "Freud and the interpretation of dreams". I have changed the Arabic language from a dialect to a literary language.

On this website: www.terezia.com, you can find the summary of two conferences: "How to live with anxiety and fear", by Rim KHOUDARY and "The inner peace", by Jina KHOUDARY. I reread these two summaries.

Boushra ARROUK sent me this conference: "From the mask to the truth". It is transcribed word for word in Arabic dialect, I modified the Arabic language, from dialect to a literary language.

In Dutch: Paul BEGUEYB S.J, Frans van der Lugt S.J 1938-2014, Bruggenbouwer en martelaar in Syrië, Nijmegen, Valkhof Pers, 2015. In French: Paul BEGUEYB S.J, Frans van der Lugt S.J 1938-2014, Bâtisseur de ponts et martyr en Syrie, éditions Valkhof Pers, 2015.

TABLE OF CONTENTS

Dépôt légal : Troisième trimestre 2022

www.ingramcontent.com/pod-product-compliance
Lightning Source LLC
Chambersburg PA
CBHW051752250726
48659CB00001B/383